MICHEÁL Ó h

# PICTURES AT THE ABBEY

The Collection of the Irish National Theatre
with a *Conversation Piece* by
Lennox Robinson
*and sixty-four illustrations, twenty-eight in colour*

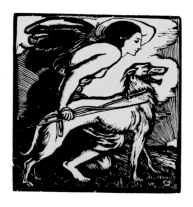

THE DOLMEN PRESS
*in association with* The Irish National Theatre Society Limited

Composed in Palatino type by Design and Art Facilities Limited
and printed in the Republic of Ireland by Irish Printers Limited

for

The Dolmen Press Limited
Mountrath, Portlaoise, Ireland

Edited and designed by Liam Miller

First published 1983

British Library Cataloguing in Publication Data:
Ó hAodha, Micheál
  Pictures at the Abbey: the collection of the Irish national theatre.
  1. Abbey Theatre – History – Pictorial Works
  I. Title     II. Robinson, Lennox.    Pictures in a theatre.
  792'.09418'35     PN2602.D82
    ISBN 0 85105 399 8 pbk
    ISBN 0 85105 418 8

# CONTENTS

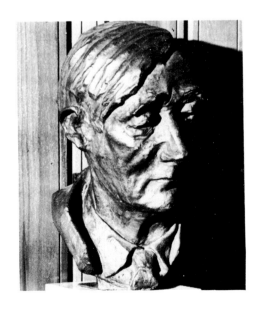

2   *Lennox Robinson* by *Garry Trimble*

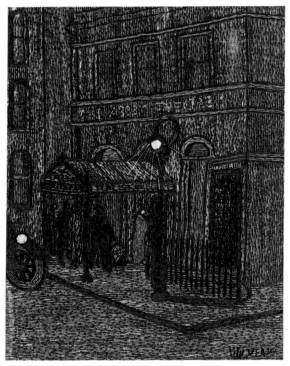

*3   The Old Abbey Theatre.* Tapestry by *Lily Yeats*

# FOREWORD

Over thirty-five years ago, Lennox Robinson published a guide to the paintings of distinguished playwrights and actors which adorned the old Abbey Theatre. Entitled *Pictures in a Theatre*, it took the form of an imaginary conversation between Lennox with his lifetime knowledge of the Abbey, and an imaginary American interested in everything appertaining to the theatre.

In a radio production of *Pictures in a Theatre* which I directed for RTE, Lennox Robinson played his inimitable self. The part of the visiting American was played by George Roy Hill, who later became famous in Hollywood as director of 'Butch Cassidy and the Sundance Kid' and other notable films.

*Pictures in a Theatre*, as Lennox wrote it, forms the central section of this book, and is introduced by some account of the theatre and the origins of its picture collection which today has ten times as many pieces as it had when the theatre opened some eighty years ago. The pictures which have come to the Abbey since Lennox Robinson wrote his piece in the 1940's are described in a third part, to bring the record up to date.

The illustrations are mostly from new photographs by Rex Roberts, and some from the archives of *Ireland of the Welcomes*, by courtesy of its Editor, Miss Elizabeth Healy. George Morrison kindly allowed us to use his unique colour transparency of Sarah Purser's stained glass in the original 1904 foyer, which remained in its original place until the fire of 1951. The transparency of Louis le Brocquy's painting of Michael Scott was kindly supplied by Mr. Kenneth M. Hay of the New York State Museum. And Karl Uhlemann kindly allowed us to include his illustrations from the 1947 edition of *Pictures in a Theatre*.

The Abbey Theatre and the Dolmen Press are indebted to the Bank of Ireland and the Knight of Glin, the Irish representative of Christies of London, who helped to make this publication possible.

Micheál Ó hAodha

7

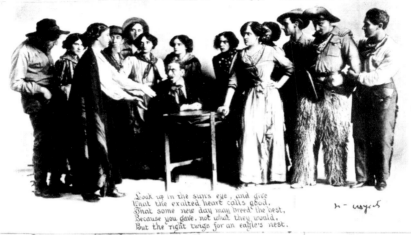

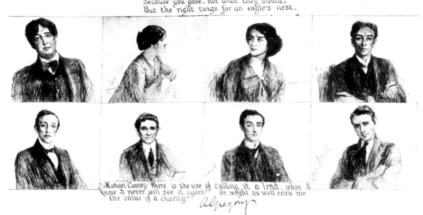

4    'The Abbey Handkerchief'. Printed Linen Square, 1913

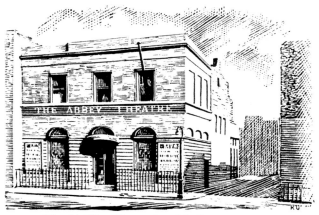

*The old Abbey Theatre from Marlborough Street*

# I

## THE THEATRE AND THE PICTURES

In her letter written in April 1904, offering the Abbey Theatre to the Irish National Theatre Company, Miss Horniman wrote, 'I can only afford to make a very little Theatre, and it must be quite simple. You all must do the rest to make a powerful and prosperous Theatre, with a high artistic ideal.' The Company's acceptance of this generous offer gave the Irish National Theatre a permanent home, one in which Yeats could create the 'household of living art' he had worked towards with all the members of the Company. Miss Horniman had made possible the purchase of the old Mechanics' Institute Theatre in Lower Abbey Street and the Penny Bank in Marlborough Street, both buildings to be converted into a home for the Company from the plans of Joseph Holloway.

Joseph Holloway, a Dublin architect with a consuming passion for theatre, was engaged by Miss Horniman to design the conversion of the buildings acquired as the original Abbey Theatre. His original estimate of cost was £1,300, and the total outlay did not exceed £1,700. This sum included the carpets supplied by Millar and Beatty, the scenery made and painted by The Irish

9

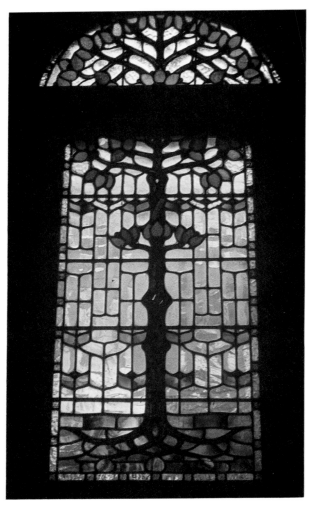

5 'The stained glass in
the entrance hall' by
Sarah Purser RHA, 1904

Decorating Company under the supervision of scenic artist
Frederick Byer, the complete electrical installation (under the
direction of W. G. Fay) erected by T. J. Sheehan, Dame Street,
Electrical Engineer and Contractor to H.M. War Department. The
painting of the building was executed by Marks Brothers of 13
South Anne Street. The Fireproof Curtain and the external
porches were the work of J. & C. McLoughlin, Art Metal Workers

and Constructional Engineers, 47 to 54 Great Brunswick Street, Dublin and the stained glass windows were supplied by An Túr Gloine, 24 Upper Pembroke Street, Dublin, Proprietor Miss Purser H.R.H.A., Manager A. E. Child.

Yeats and Miss Horniman supervised the details of the decoration of the theatre and so he could write proudly in the theatre review *Samhain*, published on the opening date of the Abbey, 27 December 1904,

> The work of decoration and alteration has been done by Irishmen, and everything, with the exception of a few articles that are not made here, or not of a good enough quality, has been manufactured in Ireland. The stained glass in the entrance hall is the work of Miss Sarah Purser and her apprentices, the large copper mirror frames are from the new metal works at Youghal, and the pictures of some of our players are by an Irish Artist. These details and some details of form and colour in the building, as a whole, have been arranged by Miss Horniman herself.

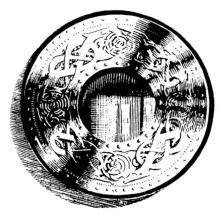

*One of the copper framed mirrors in the theatre*

The 'Irish Artist' referred to was, of course, Yeats's father, the portrait painter John Butler Yeats who, as well as portraits of the early members of the Abbey company, painted most of the significant figures in the Ireland of his time. Ten years after the opening of the Abbey he wrote from New York, where he lived

11

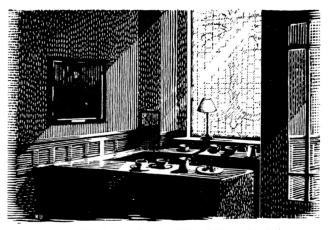

*A corner of the foyer, with one of Sarah Purser's windows*

during his last years, that 'all art begins in portraiture', and certainly the group of portraits from his hand which form the nucleus of the theatre's collection show what a fine recorder of his contemporaries he was.

The correspondent of *The Freeman's Journal* reporting the private view of the completed theatre in December 1904, gave an impression of the interior and of the original arrangement of the paintings:

> The visitor in going in finds himself in a large carpeted porch, the walls of which are hung with portraits, painted by Mr. W. B. Yeats *(sic)*, of Mr. William Fay, the stage manager of the theatre; Mr. Frank Fay, Miss Maire Nic Shiubhlaigh, and Miss Horniman, proprietress of the theatre. In the green-room at one side are portraits of Dr. Douglas Hyde and Mr. George W. Russell, Vice-Presidents of the Irish National Theatre Society, also by Mr. Yeats, and a portrait of Mr. Yeats himself, painted by Madame Troncy, of Paris.

The writer of the piece confused the Yeatses, father and son, but both must share the credit for the establishment of the collection of portraits which has continued to grow during the three-quarters of a century since the theatre opened.

Miss Purser's stained glass windows graced the foyer of the

12

Abbey until the original theatre closed after the fire which destroyed the dressing rooms and stage area in July 1951. Fortunately the collection of pictures survived and are on view in the new Abbey Theatre which was opened on 16 July 1966. Five of the seven portraits mentioned in *The Freeman's Journal* are still in the collection. The portrait of Douglas Hyde is in the National Gallery of Ireland and that of W. B. Yeats by 'Madame Troncy of Paris' cannot by traced.

The most familiar picture of this period associated with the Abbey is the emblem of the theatre, a woodcut by Elinor Monsell which Yeats commissioned at her exhibition in Dublin. This is described, probably by Yeats, in a note in a 1908 Abbey programme:

> It is the work of an Irish artist, Miss Monsell, now Mrs Darwin, and represents Queen Maeve, the heroic queen of ancient Irish legend. The dog is the Irish wolfhound, and it is not known whether it was with intention or not that Miss Monsell put into the background the raying sun, which is one of the symbols of Ireland.

The device is reproduced on the title page of this book.

The Abbey opened on 27 December 1904, in the year of *Ulysses*, but some six months postmature for a 'Bloomsday' birthday. Otherwise Joyce would surely have recorded that Mrs Bannerman Palmer as 'Hamlet' had been replaced by *The Sleeping Beauty* at the Gaiety, that the Theatre Royal had the Moody Manners Company and Mr. Joseph O'Mara in *Carmen* and that the Queen's relied on an 'Entirely New Irish Historical Drama, *Sarsfield* or *The Siege of Limerick* featuring the 'Great Irish Comedian, Mr. James O'Brien, with 'Charming Scenery, Old Irish Melodies and Beautiful Wardrobe'. But Blazes Boylan or Citizen Cusack would hardly have been satisfied. 'The Abbey had one serious fault', wrote Page Dickinson, 'it had no bar. If you wanted a drink you had to cross the street, go round the corner and get to a public house.'

Indeed it is remarkable that the Abbey was 'dry' until the night of 17 July 1951 when, to the strains of 'Keep the Home Fires Burning', the curtain fell on *The Plough and the Stars* a few hours before the theatre went up in flames. The following night, despite the loss of scenery, costumes and props, the play was staged in the Peacock Theatre next door. Later the company moved for a time to the Rupert Guinness Memorial Hall in Watling Street before leasing the Queen's Theatre, where they played until the new Abbey opened on the original site in July 1966. Appropriately, the first play staged in the new Abbey was *The Plough and the Stars*, which opened in August of that year.

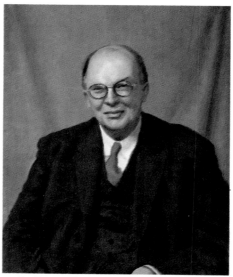

6    *Ernest Blythe* by *Sean O'Sullivan* RHA

The first theatre on the Abbey site was the Theatre Royal Opera House, built in 1820 by Frederick ('Buck') Jones. This soon became fashionable but after some years it was destroyed by fire. The Mechanics' Institute was then erected on the site to replace an earlier building in Capel Street. As this was a Temperance Hall the Institute's members, with whom temperance was not a strong point, let out the hall for political and other meetings. Among speakers there were John Mitchel, Meagher of the Sword and Smith O'Brien. When the remains of the Fenian, John O'Mahony, was refused admission to the Pro-Cathedral, the lying-in state was held there.

14

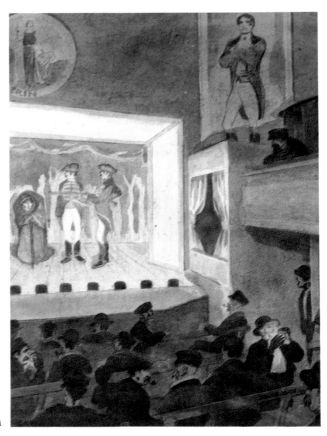

7  *'Willie Reilly'*
   *at the Old*
*Mechanics Theatre*
by *Jack B. Yeats* RHA

As The Princess's Theatre the building entered a new phase and later, under the management of a Dublin comedian, Pat Langan, became The People's Music Hall. Among its later managers were Loder Hynes and Mrs Glenville, mother of Shaun Glenville, but over the years its status gradually declined to that of a penny-gaff and at one time the hall was used as a boxing arena. Finally, in 1901, J. B. Carrickford and Madame Louise Grafton, forbears of several generations of touring 'fit-up' actors, reopened the hall as The National Theatre. They generally employed English stock actors but, as the theatre did not have a patent, their repertoire was confined to one-act pieces. The rival

15

theatre, the Queen's, objected to Carrickford's procedure and, under threat of fines of as much as £300 per night, the repertoire was changed to vaudeville and music hall. Finally the *soi-distant* National Theatre closed under pressure from the Dublin Corporation to provide elaborate safety precautions for which the site was not adequate.

When Miss Horniman acquired the lease of the property in 1904 she overcame the problem of exits by purchasing the old Penny Bank Building in Marlborough Street. This had for a time been used as the City Morgue, a fact which was not lost on the critics when they disliked a play!

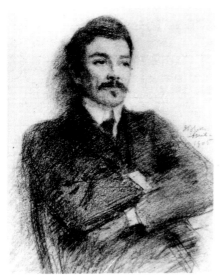

8   *J. M. Synge* by *John Butler Yeats RHA*

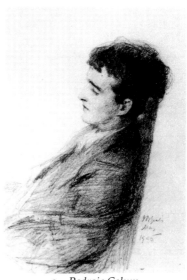

9    *Padraic Colum*
by *John Butler Yeats* RHA

The collection at the Abbey has grown over the years, often from donations of works by institutions and friends who appreciated the value of the historical associations of the theatre. Several drawings by John Butler Yeats capture the early members of the company as well as his splendid portrait in oils of Maire O'Neill.

16

Sarah Purser's portrait of Sara Allgood is there too as well as her stained glass. The later portraits form a cross section of the best of Irish twentieth century painting.

The old 'Mechanics' is represented in a fine watercolour by Jack Yeats, who also contributed as a stage 'prop' the drawing which graces the 'wanted' poster used in the early productions of Lady Gregory's *The Rising of the Moon*. Two other posters are notable – that by Beardsley for the London Avenue Theatre production of Yeats's *The Land of Heart's Desire* in 1894 in which Yeats and Miss Horniman first collaborated and from which the Irish National Theatre grew. A postcard in the Abbey archive

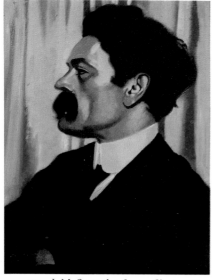

10   *J. M. Synge* by *James Sleator* RHA

# WANTED !

---

# £100 REWARD

INFORMATION required as to the whereabouts of Man of following description :---Dark hair. dark eyes, smooth face : height, five feet three.

Any information that will lead to his apprehension to be sent to D. I.

11   *"Prop" poster for* The Rising of the Moon *by Lady Gregory* by *Jack B. Yeats*

from Beardsley to Florence Farr describes the design as 'rather jolly' but his design is one of the finest posters of the eighteen nineties. The other poster design was donated by Augustus John as a contribution to the Abbey Theatre Matinee Fund in 1921. Since the opening of the new theatre in 1966 the many poster designs by Irish artists provide a representative cross section of

Irish graphic art today. Examples of these are usually on sale in the theatre.

A printed linen square, the 'Abbey handkerchief' with a photograph of the company in *The Shewing-up of Blanco Posnet* by Shaw was sold during an American tour in 1913 to raise funds for a Dublin Gallery to house Sir Hugh Lane's collection of pictures. The design also incorporates eight portrait drawings by John Butler Yeats. Hugh Lane was Lady Gregory's nephew and he bequeathed his collection of pictures to Ireland but, as the codicil to his will which confirmed the gift was not witnessed, the bequest was in dispute from the time of his death in the Lusitania sinking in 1915 until a settlement was reached in the 1950's whereby the pictures rotate between the Hugh Lane Municipal Gallery in Dublin and the Tate Gallery in London.

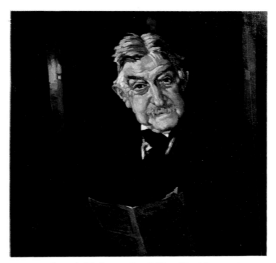

12    *Joseph Holloway* by *Lilian Davidson* RHA

The portraits at the Abbey are not confined to the actors and playwrights. Joseph Holloway, the architect of the theatre and its most persistent first-nighter during his long life, is shown in a painting by Lilian Davidson. After Holloway's death in 1944 the two hundred quarto volumes of his diary were presented to the National Library where they are a treasure trove for theatre

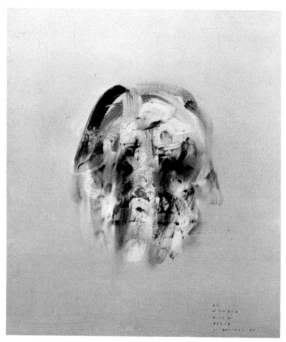

*13　Michael Scott by Louis leBrocquy RHA*

historians. There are portraits of musicians, John F. Larchet, who was musical director for many years and who set many of Yeats's lyrics to music, Seán Ó Riada who was musical director for part of his too-short life. Ernest Blythe who, as Minister for Finance, helped the provision of the first State subsidy to the theatre in 1925 and was Managing Director of the company from 1941 to 1967 is shown in a painting by Sean O'Sullivan, who also made many of the later drawings. And among the most recent additions to the collection is the painting by Louis leBrocquy of Michael Scott, the architect of the new theatre, where the 'Pictures at the Abbey' are now on permanent display.

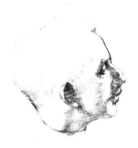

14  *Seán Ó Riada* by *Thomas Ryan* RHA

During the 1940's Lennox Robinson described the pictures then on show in the guise of an 'Imaginary Conversation' with an American student. His piece, *Pictures in a Theatre* was originally printed in *The Leader* as a series of articles and later made into a small book for the theatre by Colm O Lochlainn at the Sign of the Three Candles. Lennox described about twenty pieces then on show in the foyer and in the Green Room and the pictures he describes are reproduced with his text in the following section of this book.

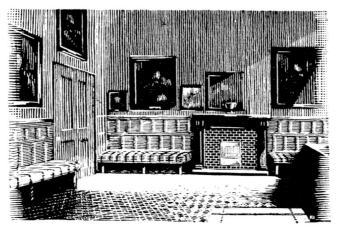

*The fireplace end of the foyer*

## II

# PICTURES IN A THEATRE

A CONVERSATION PIECE

*by*

## LENNOX ROBINSON

*Compiled from a series of articles
published in* The Leader *in 1946
and issued as a booklet by the Abbey Theatre, 1947*

*He enclosed a letter from Professor Merriam of Montana University,
Missoula. It said that Brendan O'Neill was in the American Army and, if
in luck and he survived, would come to Dublin to look up relations, and
that he was interested in the theatre and could I do anything for him? I
made an appointment one morning in the vestibule of the Abbey Theatre.
Brendan turned out to be a strapping six-footer and he brought with him
a rather weedy young man. He introduced him:*

21

BRENDAN: My second cousin, David, from Sligo, or near there.

DAVID: From the borders of Sligo and Donegal, sir.

SELF: I know Sligo fairly well and a bit of Donegal.

BRENDAN: What I want to know is, about this theatre. You see my eldest brother – he's sixteen years older than me – was at a summer school once at Missoula and you were there and you lectured about Ireland and the Abbey Theatre, and you produced a play with the students, and then a few years after he saw the Abbey Players in Helena – I don't think you were with them – and he fell for them, but my dad – he's a real old Irishman – he had seen the same sort of plays in Chicago years back and he liked the acting but he said some of the plays were terribly crude, that *Playboy*, for instance, by Synge——

SELF: Sing *(I corrected)*. You singe a cat, you sing Synge.

BRENDAN: Thanks, I accept the correction. But there was one of yours he liked, something about the Black Hills.

SELF: I'm glad he liked it.

BRENDAN: He said it was all right – I mean he liked it. Now, tell me about this theatre.

SELF: There's so much to tell, lots of books have been written about it – I've written about it so often myself. Let's start by just looking at these pictures in the hall. Don't you think it's a lovely little gallery?

BRENDAN: It certainly is. I don't pretend to know much about pictures but I——

SELF: Know what I like. Isn't that the best reason for liking a picture? So, let's just go quietly round, starting on our right – no, for the moment we'll skip the first one and look at the one over the gas-fire.

BRENDAN: She looks a fine, powerful old woman.

SELF: She *was* fine and powerful; that is Lady Gregory. There would be no theatre here, you and I woundn't be standing here, if

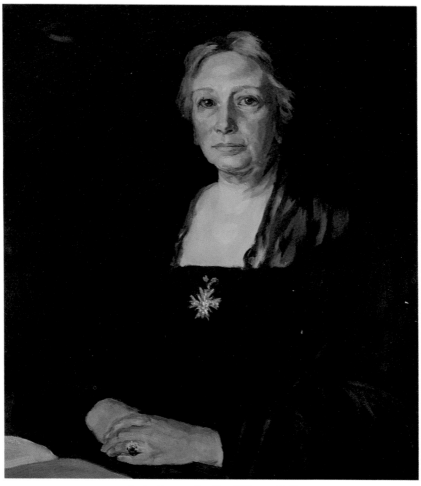

15　*Lady Gregory by Gerald Festus Kelly* RA

it wasn't for her. She was of the Protestant class – what some people sneeringly call "the ascendancy class" – and she was a great Irishwoman. She met Yeats, and she knew a man called Edward Martyn, a neighbour of her own, a Catholic landlord in County Galway. Martyn and Yeats had written plays and they

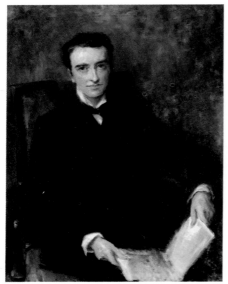 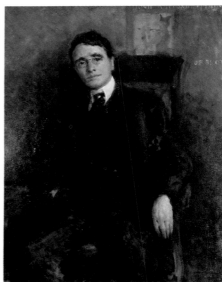

16  *Frank Fay* by *John Butler Yeats* RHA          17  *W. G. Fay* by *John Butler Yeats* RHA

wanted them produced, and they thought of having them done in London. Lady Gregory, who up to this had no particular interest in the drama, said they should be done in Dublin and, thanks to her energy, done in Dublin they were – this was back in 1899. In a few years' time she became absorbed in the Irish theatre, she started to write plays herself and ended up by being one of the most important playwrights of our early days. She was a Director of our theatre and without her firm hand and her unflinching belief in our Theatre's future we should have no national theatre in Ireland today. . . . But let's leave her for a moment, she'll crop up again and again, for she permeates every stick and stone of this building. We'll turn back – and forward – to the two young men whose portraits hang on her right and left. Their names are Fay, Frank Fay and Willie Fay.

BRENDAN: Nice-looking fellers.

SELF: Aren't they? And so beautifully painted by J. B. Yeats. He was W. B. Yeats' father and the father of Jack B. Yeats, our finest, most original painter in Ireland to-day, some think one of the

24

most exciting painters in Europe and America. But the Fays – they were brothers – were acting in small halls in Dublin, and they got to know what Yeats and Martyn were trying to do, knew they were trying to create an Irish drama, on Yeats' side a poetic, heroic drama, on Martyn's side a more psychological drama. Those early performances had been given by professional English companies, generally in some big Dublin theatre, but when the Fays and their friends joined Yeats' group a change took place. The performances were held now in small Dublin halls ill-fitted for stage purposes, the audiences were generally small and none of the players were paid. The brothers were contrasted in their gifts; Frank, a beautiful speaker of verse, Willie a comedian of genius. Can't you see the poetry in Frank's eyes?

BRENDAN: I sure can. Who's that left of the door?

SELF: That's Doctor Larchet. Not a Doctor of Medicine, a Doctor of Music. He came to the theatre, a young man, as leader of the orchestra. It was a poorly-paid job. Jack Larchet became very

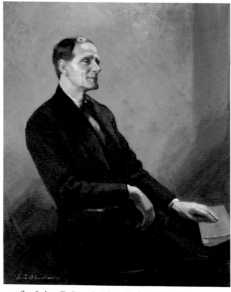

18   *John F. Larchet* by *Seán O'Sullivan* RHA

25

successful and busy; teaching, composing, university work, examinations, but he so loved the Abbey that he could not bear to leave it. He knew every play that was performed though he would always consider the acts of a play as "the interval" and his music the *coup* of the evening. And many others agreed with him and would go out for a smoke during the acts and come back for what *we* call "the interval." It's a fine portrait, very like him, and though Jack doesn't conduct for us any more I don't think he ever misses a new play. Above the door is George Russell, better known as "A.E." He had a lot to do with the Theatre in the very early days before it had a theatre, but then he dropped out of the movement.

BRENDAN: But we've missed the delicate-looking chap in the corner.

SELF: Ah, that's a man called Padraic Colum. He was one of our earliest playwrights, he started to write at about the same time as Synge, that is to say, when the theatre was beginning to turn from the poetic, heroic theatre Yeats had dreamed of to a more realistic type of play – but it had not yet reached the harshly realistic plays of T. C. Murray, R. J. Ray and myself – the "three Cork realists," as Yeats called us. He wrote about contemporary country life, the life of the small farmer, such plays as *The Land* and *The Fiddler's House,* bringing into them a poetry of speech – not as emphasised as Synge's speech – but essentially poetry. He has lived in New York for many, many years and has a distinguished literary position there, I am sure you have heard of him.

BRENDAN: I certainly have. So that's Padraic Colum?

SELF: Yes, but a long time ago. His best play, written much later than the ones I have named, was not about the country, it was about a country-town and a workhouse-master, it is called *Thomas Muskerry,* I am proud to remember that I gave it its first production.

DAVID: Who's that above the box-office, staring down?

SELF: That's W. B. Yeats, son of the man who painted the portraits and the originator of this theatre. And yet I don't think he cared very much for plays, he told me once that the only plays he really

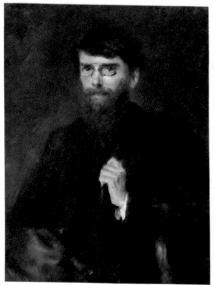

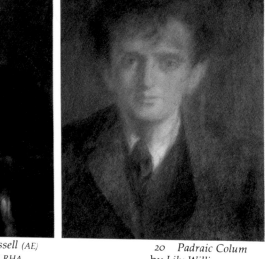

19 *George William Russell (AE)*
by *John Butler Yeats* RHA

20 *Padraic Colum*
by *Lily Williams* RHA

liked were Shakespeare's. He wrote some beautiful verse-plays himself, but when our theatre grew realistic he stood aside, though late in life he wrote a very remarkable little prose play about Jonathan Swift called *The Words Upon the Window-pane*. But he was much more a poet than a dramatist and, funny to say, a hardheaded man of business. He could even understand a balance-sheet, and that's not an easy thing to do. As you say, he stares down. I like to fancy he's watching the people booking seats and wondering whether there will be a full house tonight, and whether the ladies behind the little window are giving the correct change – I bet they are.

But now let's swing to the left, to the far corner. That lovely, delicate portrait – look at the hands – is of Miss Horniman. She was an Englishwoman who got to know Yeats and to admire his work and the work of the players, who were still only an amateur company, with no theatre, not even a hall of their own. She took

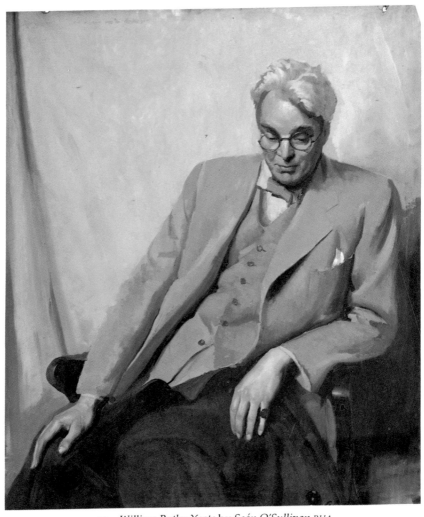

21　*William Butler Yeats* by *Seán O'Sullivan* RHA

over this old theatre, furbished it up, made additions to it and for
a number of years gave it an annual subsidy. To have a permanent
home, to have a fixed income – even if a small one – meant a
tremendous lot. The players could now be paid regular salaries –

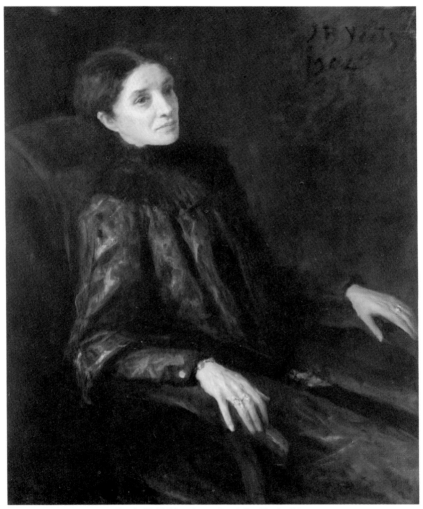

22    *Annie E. F. Horniman* by *John Butler Yeats* RHA

fantastically small salaries judged by present-day standards – but it enabled them to leave their jobs and devote all their time to the theatre. I believe she was difficult to work with – I never met her – she wrote on yellow paper in red ink, and Synge used to declare that he grew slightly ill when he saw a yellow envelope in the morning's post. But, difficult though she may have been, this theatre is deeply in her debt.

DAVID: The next is a powerful-looking chap.

SELF: Isn't he? His name was Higgins, F. R. Higgins, he was our managing-director for a few years but he wasn't, mainly, a man of the theatre. He was a poet, our best, most promising poet – no, I shouldn't say promising, for he was a poet of achievement and a great friend of Yeats. Alas, he died all too young. I can never look at that splendid portrait by Seán O'Sullivan without a deep pang of regret.

BRENDAN: It seems just too bad. And the guy beyond him, isn't that yourself?

SELF: That guy, as you say, is indeed myself. We needn't dwell on the subject of the portrait but only note the rich beauty of the painting. It is by a man called Sleator, one of our finest portrait painters, he was made President of our Hibernian Academy a few

23    *F. R. Higgins* by *Sean O'Sullivan* RHA

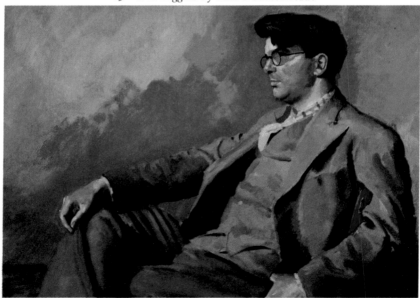

months ago. But now before starting up the stairs, what about going out for a cup of coffee and a cigarette?

BRENDAN: Sounds O.K. by me.

DAVID: I'd like that – or a bottle of stout.

SELF: Right. Let's go.

*(And we went)*

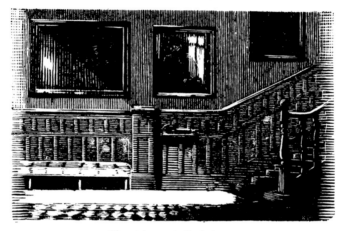

*The staircase to the balcony*

## II

SELF: Well, here we are back again. There are not many pictures left for us to look at – only five – but I've a lot to tell you about them . . . just one step up the stairs and you'll see it better.

BRENDAN: I don't care a lot for it.

SELF: You're quite right, it's the only poor picture in the hall. It was painted by an old Irishwoman – at least she was old when she died, ninety something – her name was Sarah Purser, a rich, witty old woman and she could paint very good pictures and some not so good; and this is one of her not-so-goods, but when she offered the portrait to us we were delighted to accept it, for our gallery

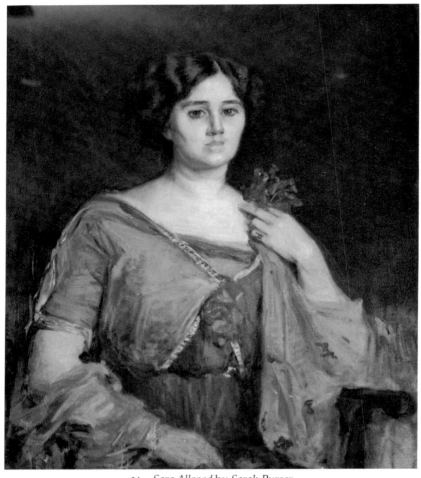

24    *Sara Allgood* by *Sarah Purser*

wouldn't be complete if there wasn't in it a portrait of Sara Allgood.

BRENDAN: Gee! Is that Sara Allgood. I've heard a lot about her.

SELF: Of course you have. I don't think we've ever had an actress

32

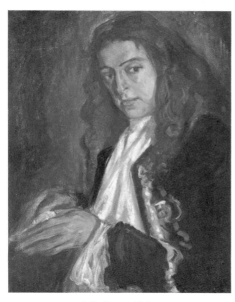

*25   Arthur Sinclair as King James I in* The White Cockade *by Lady Gregory by Robert Gregory*

to compare with her. Of course, every great player is unique and, in a sense, it is ridiculous to make comparisons, but Sara Allgood was peculiarly unique. (I speak in the past tense because it is years since she played here, but she is still very much alive, thank God.) To begin with, she had a marvellous voice. You have heard of Sarah Bernhardt's "Voice of Gold"; I only heard the French Sarah in her old age and her voice then did not particularly impress me, other things about her did, immensely. But our

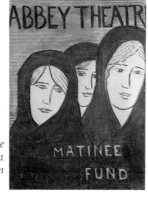

*26   Poster for the Matinee Fund, 1921 by Augustus John*

Sara's voice had a range, a depth, a clarity impossible to describe. It was gold and silver and, if she so wished, iron.

BRENDAN: A gift of God, I guess.

SELF: Yes, but God gave her, as it were, just the ingredients, it was for herself to fashion and mould and use them. How often have I known her to get to the theatre an hour before rehearsal and, standing alone on the stage, practise her vocal exercises to a theatre empty save for the chars. Consequently, eventually, she had perfect control of her voice which I admit must have begun as something wonderful, but it was her own hard work which made it unique. But don't think she was just a fine speaker, she is an actress to her finger-tips, a mistress of comedy as well as of tragedy. She created the part of "Juno" in *Juno and the Paycock.* That is a Dublin slum play and the Dublin slum accent is not very beautiful but to that part she brought all her motherly instincts – she was always a perfect mother on the stage, a tender mother, a domineering mother, oh, she could be harsh if the part demanded harshness and she made "Juno" a thing to be long remembered. And what humour she had! I wish you could have seen her in some of Lady Gregory's early comedies, in *The Jackdaw* or *Hyacinth Halvey.* Lady Gregory loved dearly and she adored Lady Gregory. Dear Sally! How she and I used to fight in the old days.

DAVID: About what?

BRENDAN: Yes. What did you scrap about?
SELF: Oh, the silliest little things, I've forgotten them, the things actresses *do* scrap about. But we forgave and forgot very quickly. She "made" my first two plays so I should never have said a cross word to her.

BRENDAN: And she's not here now?

SELF: No, she's in Hollywood, worse luck. You Americans have taken so many of our good players, Barry Fitzgerald, J. M. Kerrigan, Arthur Shields – we mustn't grudge you them, they are earning what they deserve and we have as good a company as ever we had, but if Sara Allgood walked on the stage this evening what a cheer there'd be, you'd hear it down to the Liffey. One often sees her on the screen, but I have never seen her yet in a part worthy of her genius. She's happy in Hollywood, has a little house of her own and hens and she drives her car – my, I wouldn't trust myself in a car with Sally at the wheel; why, when she was trying to learn to ride a bicycle, practising behind the Custom House, her teacher advised her to give it up, he said she would be a menace to the public. I get long letters from her now and then and she sends me tea – Again, bless her. . . . Now, a step up.

BRENDAN: A man.

DAVID: In a sort of a fancy dress.

SELF: Yes, that's Arthur Sinclair, a contemporary of Sara Allgood's. When those two were acting together and you had Kerrigan and Fred O'Donovan and Maire O'Neill and Sydney Morgan in the other parts then you would have a performance to make you sit up and remember and remember. The "fancy dress," David, is because the artist painted Sinclair as "King James" in a play of Lady Gregory's called *The White Cockade*. The picture was painted by her son, Robert, a beautiful painter, killed flying over Italy in the last war, not this one. Sinclair was – is – a great actor. He is known best to the public as a comedian, yet grand and rich as his comedy is, I like almost better to remember his tragic parts. In a little play called *The Pie-dish*, as a brutal farmer in a play of mine called *The Cross Roads*, above all as the blind man in *The Well of the Saints*. He has not Sara Allgood's lovely voice, but he has all her versatility – perhaps he is even more versatile than she is. He acts often in London and I read grand notices of his performances but I haven't seen him act for years. That striking drawing at the top of the stairs is by the English artist, Augustus John. Years ago, in 1921, when we were deep in the Anglo-Irish war things went very hard with the Theatre, we had a curfew at half-past eight, and to raise money to keep us alive an Irish friend of ours, J. B. Fagan, arranged a series of lectures in his great drawingroom in London. Yeats lectured, and Shaw came and read the first act – it had not yet been played or published – of *Back to Methusaleh*. We made quite a lot of money and Augustus John gave us this drawing to be auctioned. Fagan said wittily enough that it depicts

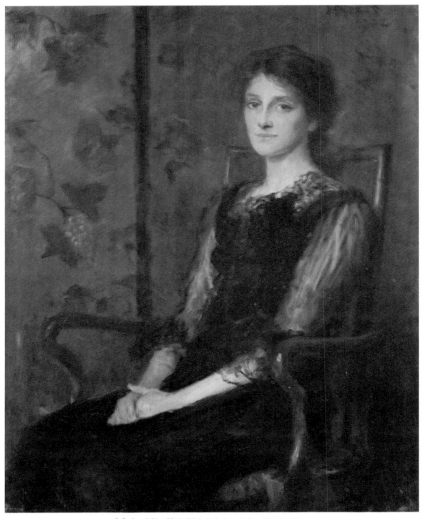

*27    Maire Nic Shiubhlaigh* by *John Butler Yeats* RHA

Sara Allgood and her sister Maire O'Neill not allowing the new
actress to have a look-in. Yes, I'm afraid actresses are often like
that, not always. Actors are generally much more generous. But
now, look across – no, we'll go downstairs and look at them from
the floor.

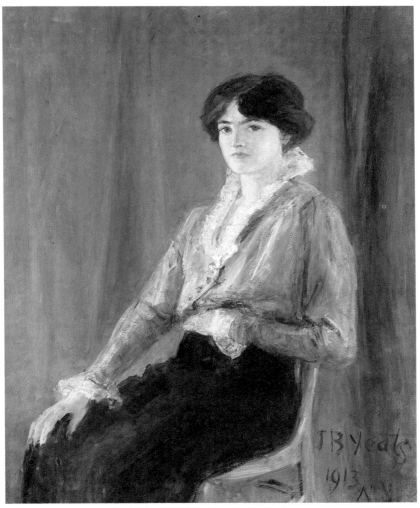

*28   Maire O'Neill by John Butler Yeats* RHA

DAVID: Two grand women. The top one's a beauty.

SELF: You're right. Her name is Maire nic Shiubhlaigh. She was one of the earliest and the best of our actresses. She lacked the power of Sara Allgood and she hadn't the *diablérie* of Sara's sister,

Maire O'Neill, hanging below her, but she had a grace and a charm and a poetic beauty that was all her own. I never knew her well as an actress, she was a little before my time, but we meet fairly often and she doesn't seem to have lost a fraction of her delicacy and charm. Yeats painted it, oh, many years ago, it's a very poetic picture, don't you think? The portrait hanging below is by him also, painted years later in New York.

BRENDAN: I guess the girls were different.

SELF: They certainly were. Maire O'Neill – she is Sara Allgood's sister – how can I describe her? That is the heart-breaking thing about acting, it is made afresh each night, and each night perishes like a soap-bubble. Colley Cibber said it so much better than I can when he wrote two hundred years ago trying to describe the great Betterton in Shakespeare. "The animated graces of the player can live no longer than the instant breath and motion that presents them; or at best can but faintly glimmer through the memory or imperfect attestation of a few surviving spectators," Maire O'Neill doesn't "faintly glimmer" through my memory. She is as vivid as when I saw her in *The Shadow of the Glen,* the first night I was ever in this theatre, October 8th, 1908 – the night of my first play here. She was beautiful, dark, very Irish-looking. Her qualities were quite different to her sister's. When I came to the Theatre first there was a certain rivalry between them, there needn't have been, Sally could do things Molly couldn't touch, and vice-versa. Sally's tragedy was grandiose, Molly's was intimate and personal. She could be deliciously impish. In her Pegeen Mike (in *The Playboy,* that play your father so disliked) she ran through the whole scale of the emotions, she was practical, harsh, playful, loving – everything a young girl can be, right up to her last heart-broken cry. I don't believe there will ever be such a Pegeen Mike again. She acted with every fibre of her body. I have seen her standing in the wings waiting for her cue, cigarette in her mouth, a girl, whispering gaily, raddled and dressed as an old woman but still a girl; then the cue came, the cigarette was crushed out and in an instant every muscle in her body seemed to alter, her face shaped itself exactly to those lines which had looked so absurd, the young voice cracked and she hobbled on to the stage an old Cork country woman. She was a bit of a divil (which is not the

38

same thing I'd have you know, Mr. MacNeill, as being a *devil*).
Men were crazy after her and she went on tour one summer in
England – not with our company – and vowed she'd come back
with three engagement rings – and did.

BRENDAN: I'm not surprised.

SELF: Well, that's the end of our little picture-show.

BRENDAN: Is that all there is?

SELF: We haven't room to hang any more here. Of course there's
a lot of stuff in the Green Room.

DAVID: Oh, couldn't we——?

BRENDAN: It would be fine – if it's not taking too much of your
time.

SELF: Not at all, if you'd really care to.

BRENDAN: If we'd care!

SELF: Very well. We'll go through this door and across the stage,
I don't think they're rehearsing this morning. Mind the steps. I'll
go first and hold the door open . . . I *told* you to mind the steps!


### III

SELF: Well, you haven't sprained an ankle . . . I'll switch on a light.
I'm glad Dossy Wright isn't here. He hates my finger on a switch.
He's always got his eye on the electric light bill, and, of course,
rightly.

BRENDAN: But, gosh, this isn't the stage?

SELF: Yes, it is—

BRENDAN: But – but – it doesn't go anywhere.

SELF: No – it's only about twelve or fourteen feet deep– I've no
head for figures: you see there's a lane just behind – we can't get
more depth but one of these days, and really within a few years,

39

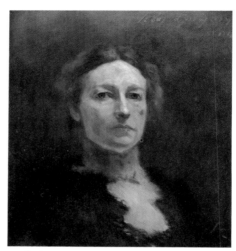

*29   Lady Gregory by AE (George William Russell)*

we'll have a new grand theatre – I suppose some of us old Abbey stagers will regret the passing of this pocket-handkerchief of a stage – I can't think without emotion of all the grand plays and the grand players who have trod these boards. Ah, there will be just as good players and plays to come. But, you see, we've quite a good deal of space here on the far side of the stage – room for props and scenery. If players were nearly always friends of mine, the stage staff were always friends, I can't remember a decent row between us. I like to dwell on their names; sometimes they must be only *in memoriam*; I mean, because they are dead, but others, thank goodness, are very much alive. But in memory, dear Barney Murphy, I think the best prompter we ever had, though once I, myself, was supposed to be a good prompter.

BRENDAN: Are there good and bad prompters? I thought you just spat out the words.

SELF: It's not quite as easy as that – you need to know when a player has really dried up. If the sentence is "I forget" you spit (as you say) "I forget, I *forget*" until at last the player says in

40

desperation "Yes, I know I forget." But there was a time when Sally Allgood wouldn't go on in a new part unless I was crouching at the back of the fire ready to help her. But then this corner of the stage is so full of memories. But of course, topping everyone, Seaghan Barlow. How afraid of him I was 35 years ago. I think I am a bit afraid of him still. His lunch of cocoa and his study of Greek, his telling you that what you asked for was perfectly impossible, and the next day the impossible was in your hands. The scenery and furniture, you see, is only a small bit of what we use – a repertory theatre has to accumulate so much scenery – and the costumes. We won't go upstairs to see Miss Devoy – I'm not afraid of her – she has an infallible memory. I will say to her vaguely "There was that pale green silk dress – twenty-five years ago, very pale——" and Miss Devoy will go into a dream and tomorrow the dress will be there. But we haven't yet got near the Green Room. You see I could talk for hours about the workers. Come up these steps, I haven't much time.

*(We enter)*

THE GREEN ROOM PHOTOGRAPHS

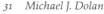

*30   Barry Fitzgerald*                    *31   Michael J. Dolan*

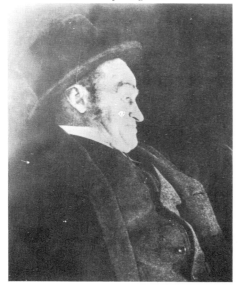
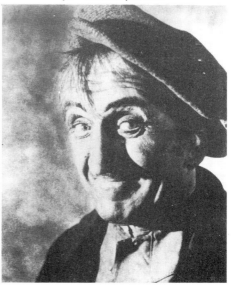

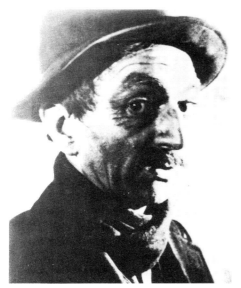

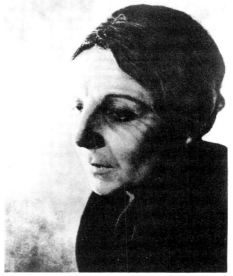

*32    F. J. McCormick*                    *33    Eileen Crowe*

*34    Maureen Delany*                    *35    Arthur Shields*

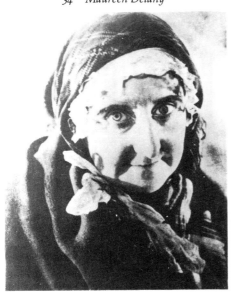

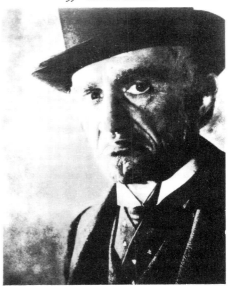

BRENDAN: *(Coming in):* It's really a Green Room?

SELF: Yes, so few theatres nowadays have a Green Room. I mean a room where players can sit down and talk with each other, perhaps play a game of cards or darts while waiting for the third act. I think I shouldn't have bothered you to bring you around for there is really nothing very distinguished to show you. But you see those clever photographs? Those are of the players you were seeing in the play last night. Eileen Crowe, I often think a better "Juno" than Sara Allgood because more "slum" without the poetry which Sara couldn't resist bringing into the part. And F. J. McCormick – of course, the best actor we ever had – yes, I'm not forgetting Barry Fitzgerald and Fred O'Donovan and Arthur Sinclair, but one week he is *Joxer* and the next week *King Lear* or *Oedipus*. Ah, "there's richness for you." Oh, now you'd be bored if I went from photograph to photograph praising every one because I must praise them all. May Craig, Arthur Shields, Maureen Delany – all these lovely geniuses of players I have worked with so many years.

BRENDAN: But those others are four powerful photos.

SELF: Yes. They were taken by a man called Pirie MacDonnell, a

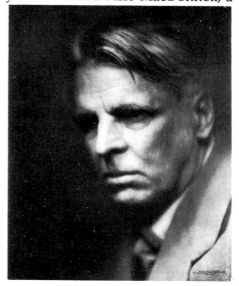

*36   W. B. Yeats, photograph
      by Pirie MacDonnell*

Scot of New York. He died a few years ago. He photographed Yeats, A.E., Colum (you saw his portrait in the vestibule), and myself. Pirrie would only photograph men, and was independent. President Hoover commended him to the White House, Pirrie declined the invitation as he wasn't interested in Hoover's face and he wasn't interested in his politics.

BRENDAN: The room seems so full of junk.

SELF: I suppose it *is* junk, but always important junk. Those presses are all crammed with scripts of plays and parts, as hard to keep correct as scenery and props and wardrobe. But there are a few important pictures in the room – a rare portrait – an early one of Lady Gregory over the fire – rare because I think it's the only portrait A.E. ever did, and then this grand portrait by Dermod O'Brien of Barry Fitzgerald as the King in *The Golden Apple*. It is my property but, of course, it is better it should hang here than in my small home – and round the corner, in the room I hold my acting classes, is a noble painting of Fred O'Donovan as Robert Emmet, painted years ago by James Sleator.

BRENDAN: I suppose there have been lots of plays about Emmet.

SELF: Not as many as you might think and perhaps none of them very good. My play about him, *The Dreamers*, wasn't the best, but

*37 Barry Fitzgerald in*
The Golden Apple *by Lady Gregory*
by *Dermod O'Brien* RHA

*38 Michael J. Dolan and Barry*
*Fitzgerald in* The Devil's Disciple
*by Bernard Shaw* by *Dermod O'Brien* RHA

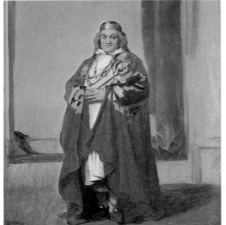

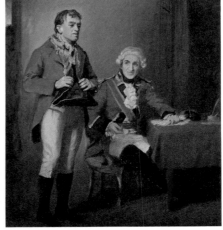

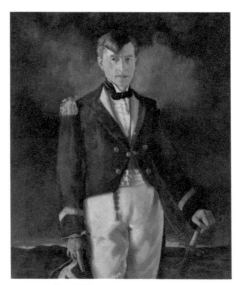

*39   Fred O'Donovan as Robert Emmet*
*in* The Dreamers *by Lennox Robinson*
*by James Sleator* RHA

it attempted to say history realistically – I mean I didn't wave a flag – of course, I was only copying the headline Lady Gregory set in her Folk History Plays. But looking at Barry Fitzgerald, and thinking of Fred O'Donovan, I think how differently they achieved fame. Fred O'Donovan from the moment of his first appearance on the stage was an actor *par excellence*. I don't mean to say that he didn't improve and enrich himself, that he didn't go from strength to strength, but he didn't have to grope and stumble for a couple of years as so many players have to do. Barry had to grope and stumble and then suddenly shone out. I don't think McCormick had to grope, but he had some stage experience before I started to work with him. But Eileen Crowe, in her early days, nearly broke my heart.

BRENDAN: You fell for her?

SELF: No. I'd often liked to have fallen *on* her and beaten her hard. She took her work so carelessly, an hour and a half lateness for a rehearsal was nothing to her. How often have I not longed to tell her off fiercely, but – oh, from the first audition she gave me, I

45

knew we had an actress and a voice and then suddenly she knew she was an actress, pulled up her socks and worked like a demon at her profession – worked as a player must work. But now I've babbled on too long, but I could go on talking about these players, these plays, these workers for hours more – and I'm boring you.

AN INTERRUPTER: A parcel for you, Mr. Robinson; eight-pence to pay.

SELF: Oh, Sloan, what is it about? Oh, I know. It is those raisins my brother is sending me from Pretoria.

SLOAN: I don't think it is from Pretoria, Mr. Robinson. It seems to me to come from Holywood from Miss Sara Allgood and it is 2 lbs. of tea.

SLEF: You see, I wasn't lying when I said that Sara Allgood sends me tea, and, of course, one of the pounds must go for Christmas to Mrs. Martin, one of our best workers, who, like all good Irishwomen, loves tea. And I'll ask tonight if Seaghan Barlow would like a pound of tea, and if he does both of them will drink it in memory of Sara Allgood and Lady Gregory. But here's Mr. Dermody coming in and he is having a rehearsal so we must clear out.

BRENDAN: It was nice and homely you knowing Montana.

SELF: Ah, isn't it far away? You know, when I was at Missoula that summer everyone was so kind. Professor, students, everyone, but sometimes I'd get very homesick for Ireland. I'd remember about 3,000 miles of sea from Ireland to New York and then about 3,000 miles of train from New York to the Rockies – would I ever arrive home again? And then, in Butte, with Professor Merriam I went down a copper mine, 3,000 feet down (not miles) and there in the dripping heat, the mines' lowest level I was greeted in soft West Cork accents with "Do you know Drimoleague? Have you ever been in Clonakilty?" Household names to me. So, perhaps, you, Brendan, felt a scrap of what I felt when you know that I can talk to you of Montana, ah – Mr. Dermody, we're interrupting – good-bye – good luck – remember me to Professor Merriam when you get back, and maybe next summer I'll get again to Sligo, Sean. . . .

46

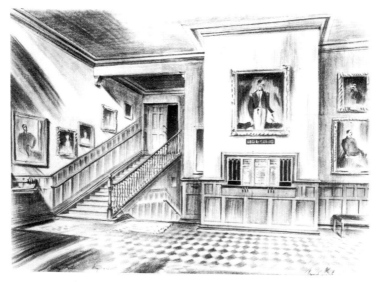

40   *The old Abbey Theatre foyer* by *Raymond McGrath* RHA

## III

## THE ABBEY THEATRE COLLECTION TODAY

Since Lennox Robinson's little book appeared in the 'forties, the collection of pictures at the Abbey Theatre has continued to expand. Pictures and sculptures have been given to the collection by friends of the theatre and the Directors have also acquired several pieces which depict members of the company whose work has continued to make Ireland's National Theatre as famous today as in the early years when the picture collection was begun by W.B. Yeats.

Today, the collection includes some 50 paintings and drawings as well as 4 sculptures, all preserved in the new Abbey Theatre building, opened in 1966 to replace the original theatre which was closed after a fire in 1951. The foyer and green room described by Lennox Robinson, with Sarah Purser's stained glass windows, no longer exist, but the new theatre, built to the design of Michael Scott, has a spacious foyer and a first floor lounge where a comprehensive selection from the pictures in the

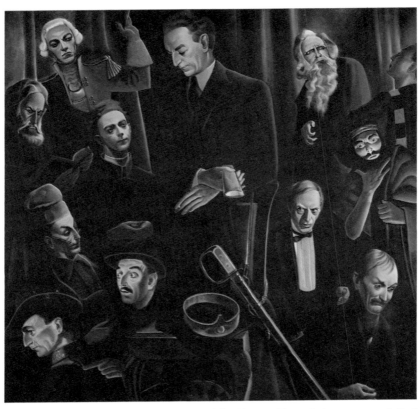

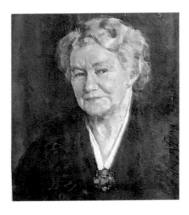

41 *'The Vacant Throne', in memory of F. J. McCormick* by *Cecil Ffrench Salkeld* RHA. The characters portrayed are, reading clockwise from bottom left, Captain Brennan in *The Plough and the Stars* (film); Shell in the film *Odd Man Out;* Peter in *The Canavans* by Lady Gregory; Don José Maria in Sierra's *The Two Shepherds;* the title role in *John Ferguson* by St John Ervine; General Burgoyne in Shaw's *The Devil's Disciple; King Lear;* Pilate in *The Story Brought by Brigid* by Lady Gregory; *Oedipus the King* in Yeats's version; the butler in the film *Hungry Hill* and Fluther Good in *The Plough and the Stars.*

42 *May Craig* by *James leJeune*

collection is always on view, forming an interesting display to visitors to the building and to audiences at the performances. As well as the pictures on show in these public areas, more of the collection is hung in the Green Room and in the rehearsal areas, a tradition which goes back to the theatre's beginning. The management is always happy to show these pictures to interested persons, by prior arrangement.

As well as Sleator's portrait which he mentioned in his essay, Lennox Robinson is also represented by a bronze bust by Garry Trimble which was presented by the Dublin Theatre Festival Council as tribute to a man whose whole life had been dedicated to the theatre as playwright, manager and director, historian of the theatre, and sometimes actor.

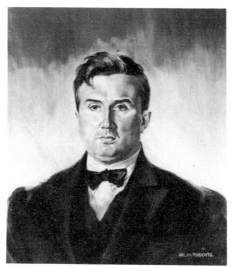

*43   Brinsley MacNamara by Hilda Roberts*

Another man of letters and playwright who served on the Abbey board, but resigned in protest at the staging of Sean O'Casey's controversial play, *The Silver Tassie* was Brinsley MacNamara, who is represented by a portrait in oils by Hilda Roberts. His best known and often revived play, *Look at the Heffernans,* was first staged in the same year as *The Plough and the Stars* (1926).

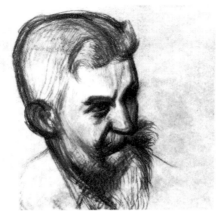

44  *George Bernard Shaw* by *William Rothenstein*

John Butler Yeats painted an oil portrait of J. M. Synge which is not in the theatre collection, but which may be seen at the National Gallery of Ireland. His drawing of the playright which is in the collection is complemented by a portrait in oil by James Sleator which captures a familiar aspect of 'that melancholy man'.

Shaw is represented in the Abbey collection by a fine *conté* drawing by William Rothenstein and a bronze bust by Epstein, presented to the Abbey players by Cyril Cusack. This stands in the Green Room, commemorating the long friendly relationship Shaw had with the theatre, and his admiration for the Abbey style of acting.

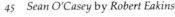

45  *Sean O'Casey* by *Robert Eakins*

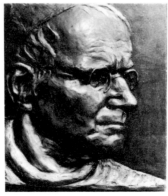

50

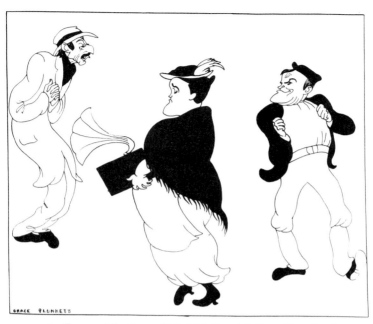

*46 'Juno and the Paycock'. F. J. McCormick, Sara Allgood and Barry Fitzgerald. Cartoon by Grace Vandeleur Plunkett*

The Abbey has yet to acquire a formal portrait of Sean O'Casey. A fine bas relief by the American sculptor, Robert Eakins was presented to the theatre in 1981 by Robert G. Lowery, editor of the *Sean O'Casey Review* and this hangs in the theatre lounge. Some of O'Casey's characters are shown in the many photographs of early performances preserved in the archives, and in witty cartoons by Grace Vandaleur Plunkett, which also picture the early company in plays by Synge and Lady Gregory.

May Craig was a legend among Abbey actresses. She played in the first productions of both *The Playboy of the Western World* in 1907 and *The Plough and the Stars* in 1926, and is also remembered as the creator of the part of the medium in *The Words Upon the Window-pane* by W.B. Yeats in 1930, and continued as a member of the company to the end of her life. She is represented in the collection by a portrait by James leJeune presented by Scott, Tallon and Walker, Architects. Another actress who appeared in the original *Plough and the Stars* cast, Shelah Richards, can be

51

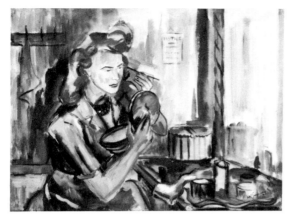

47 *Shelah Richards*
by *Norah McGuinness*

seen in a fine painting by Norah McGuinness. Her career in Irish theatre as an independent producer included the first production of one of O'Casey's later plays. She worked in Irish television for some years and returned to direct a revival of *The Plough and the Stars* in the new Abbey. Norah McGuinness, the painter, also had a long connection with the Abbey. She designed costumes and settings for Yeats plays in the 1920's, and in 1969 also designed the memorable Abbey production of *Waiting for Godot* by Samuel Beckett. Her portrait of Shelah Richards was presented to the Abbey by Switzers.

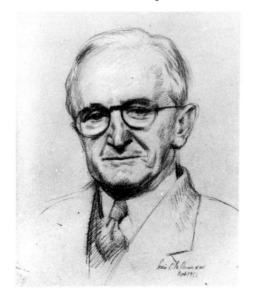

48 *Michael J. Dolan* by *Seán O'Sullivan* RHA

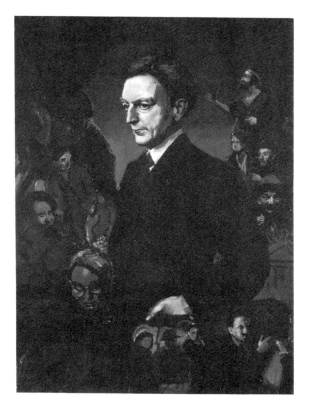

*49   F. J. McCormick by Seán O'Sullivan RHA*

Among the actors caricatured by Grace Plunkett was F.J.
McCormick who, in his years in the company portrayed over four
hundred characters. His real name was Peter Judge, and he acted
at the Abbey from 1918 until his death in 1947. He also played in
several films and is probably most widely known from his performance in Carol Reed's classic film about Belfast, *Odd Man Out*.
There are two paintings in the collection showing F.J. McCormick
in some of his most famous roles, one by Sean O'Sullivan, which
also shows Yeats, O'Casey and the Abbey emblem, and the other,
entitled 'The Vacant Throne' by Cecil ffrench Salkeld was
presented to the Abbey in memory of the actor. Another portrait
by Seán O'Sullivan is his drawing of Michael J. Dolan.

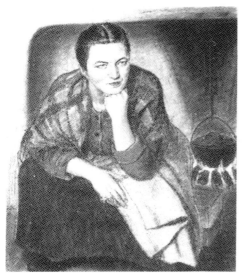 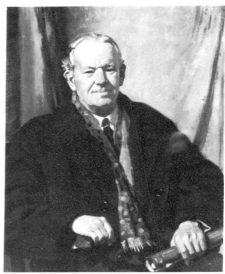

*50    Ria Mooney* by *Gaetano de Gennaro*     *51    Rutherford Mayne* by *James Sleator* RHA

A link with the theatre movement in Ulster is reflected by Sleator's portrait of the playwright and actor Rutherford Mayne (pseudonym of Samuel Waddell) who was a founder member of the Ulster Literary Theatre and later had several plays produced at the Abbey. As an actor his most noted creation was the title role of *The Emperor Jones* by Eugene O'Neill, at the Abbey in 1927.

Another Abbey player who is remembered for her great acting in a Eugene O'Neill play, *Long Day's Journey into Night* – a performance which came at the end of a long career of fine characterisations – was Ria Mooney. She created the original Rosie Redmond in *The Plough and the Stars* in 1926 and from then devoted her life to all aspects of theatre, as player, as director and as teacher of stage technique. Her portrait painted by Gaetano de Gennaro, shows her in another of her notable roles, that of The Widow Quin in *The Playboy of the Western World* by J.M. Synge. Ria Mooney's portrait was presented to the collection by Charles J. Haughey T.D., who, as Minister for Finance, provided the funding for the new theatre.

54

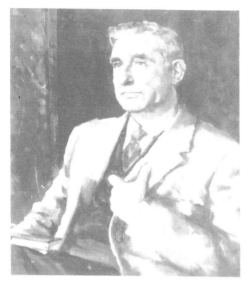

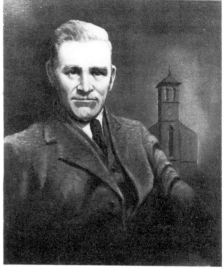

*52   Gabriel Fallon by James leJeune*          *53   George Shiels by Jack Wilkinson*

James LeJeune's portrait of Gabriel Fallon recalls another Abbey stalwart who, as an actor in the 1920's appeared in the original production of some of Sean O'Casey's plays, and as critic and historian recorded four decades of Irish theatre history. In his later life he became a member of the board of the Theatre, and was for some time Chairman.

Of the Abbey playwrights in the period after O'Casey left to live in England the most popular was undoubtedly George Shiels. His writing links the Abbey and the Ulster theatre movement, as did the writing and acting of Rutherford Mayne, StJohn Ervine and Joseph Tomelty. George Shiels was born outside Ballymoney in County Antrim in 1881. As a young man he was incapacitated for life by a railway accident in Canada, and only saw one play of his performed. He contributed over twenty plays to the repertoire, including some of the most popular pieces performed by the company, such as *The Rugged Path* and *The New Gossoon*. His portrait, by the Ulster painter, Jack Wilkinson, was presented to the Abbey by the Committee of the Ballymoney

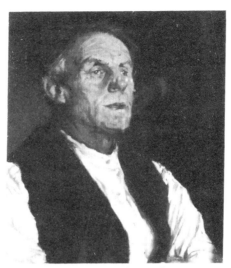

54   *Harry Brogan* by *Thomas Ryan* RHA

Drama Festival to celebrate the centenary of his birth in 1981.

Harry Brogan's characterisation of many of the roles in George Shiels' plays, as well as his playing in the great O'Casey parts will long be remembered. He graduated from the small touring companies, the 'fit-ups' to become for some thirty years one of the finest character actors in the Abbey company. His portrait, painted by Thomas Ryan RHA, was presented to the theatre by Dr. Dermot Roden in memory of this much loved actor.

Hugh Hunt came to the Abbey as producer in 1934, at the invitation of W.B. Yeats. He left after four years to work in New York, and subsequently founded the Bristol Old Vic, before becoming director of the Old Vic in London. After a period in Australia, he returned to the Abbey in 1967 and was Artistic Director of the theatre from 1969 to 1971. In 1979 he published his history of *The Abbey Theatre*. He is represented in the collection by a fine portrait by Seán O'Sullivan.

The portrait of Myles na gCopaleen by his painter brother Micheál Ó Nualláin was appropriately presented to the theatre by Guinness Ireland Limited. Written as by Myles na gCopaleen, his play *Faustus Kelly* was produced in 1943, and an adaptation of his classic in Irish, *An Béal Bocht*, has been staged twice in the new

56

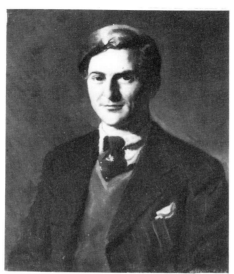

*55    Hugh Hunt by Sean O'Sullivan* RHA

Peacock theatre. An adaptation of his *At Swim-Two-Birds,* written under his other pseudonym, Flann O'Brien was also produced at the Peacock. And it is in the new Peacock foyer that the death mask of James Joyce, inspirer of Myles, as of many other writers, presented by the theatre's architect, Michael Scott is displayed. Michael Scott, originally an Abbey actor, left his theatre career to become one of Ireland's finest twentieth century architects, and is the designer of the present complex which houses both Abbey and Peacock theatres. He is represented in the collection by a characteristic head study by Louis le Brocquy.

Finally, two memorabilia bring us back to the theatre's beginnings:

Before the Abbey theatre came into being, its forerunner, the Irish National Dramatic Society, under the direction of Frank and Willie Fay, presented *Deirdre,* a play in three acts by AE, at the Camden Street Hall, on 2 April 1902, in a double bill with the first production of Cathleen Ni Houlihan by W.B. Yeats. AE, who also produced and designed his own play, painted a scene from the wings, showing Maire Quinn as Deirdre and Maire Nic Shiubhlaigh, to whom he dedicated and presented the picture, as Lavarcham. The picture was acquired from Maire Nic

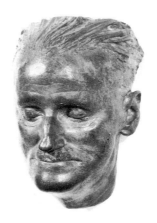

*56   James Joyce. Death mask by Paul Speck*

Shiubhlaigh's nephew, Edward Kenny, and presented to the theatre by the Bank of Ireland in 1980.

The famous copper beech tree at Coole Park on which Lady

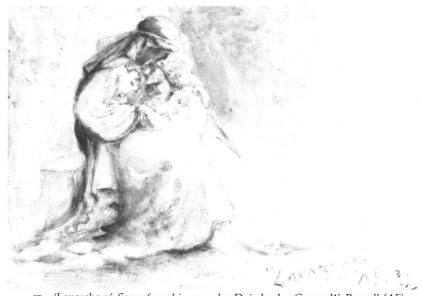

*57   'Lavarcham'. Scene from his own play* Deirdre *by George W. Russell (AE)*

58

Gregory's visitor incised their initials has become a symbol for that haven in the West of Ireland enjoyed by so many of the makers of Ireland's theatrical heritage. The then Minister for Forestry and Fisheries, Mr Tom Fitzpatrick TD, presented a fibreglass replica by Fergus O'Farrell of that section of the tree-trunk which bears the initials, to the Abbey in 1981, and, in memory of her grandson, the family presented a list in Lady Gregory's own handwriting of some of her guests whose initials are carved on the tree.

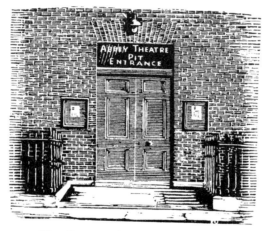

*The pit entrance in Lower Abbey Street*

# IV
## A LIST OF THE PICTURES REPRODUCED

[A] Subject Listing. Dimensions are given in centimetres, height first.

61

THE GREEN ROOM PHOTOGRAPHS

The device of the Abbey Theatre, 'Queen Maeve with wolfhound', *by* Elinor Monsell, woodcut, original size 15×14 cms, 1904, is reproduced on the title page.

Six drawings by Karl Uhlemann, first printed as illustrations to *Pictures in a Theatre* by Lennox Robinson, 1947, are reproduced by kind permission of the artist:

## [B]   Index of Artists.